HEXHAM
BLANCH LAND

by
Stewart Bonney

CONTENTS

Acknowledgments: Research assistance John Steele, Andrew Rutter, Edwin Grieve, John Watson, Cath Futers. Photography Doug Hall, John Steele.

Published by The Northumbrian Magazine – Powdene Publicity, Unit 17 St Peter's Wharf, Newcastle upon Tyne NE6 1TZ.

Printed by Creative Design & Print Ltd., Washington.

CHAPTER ONE

COASTAL DRIVE

Starting in Amble and travelling north along the coastline to Beadnell.

AMBLE

This town which lies at the mouth of the River Coquet, on the southern boundary of the Northumberland Heritage Coast, owes its existence to a violent storm in 1764.

Swollen by torrential rain, the river which had until then flowed into the North Sea half a mile to the north, broke through the low lying dunes close to the tiny hamlet of Amble.

Enterprising local businessmen were quick to grasp the opportunity presented by the river's change of course and following an Act of Parliament in 1837, work began on the construction of a large new harbour which soon became one of the country's busiest coal ports.

By the end of the 19th century this bustling harbour was handling 7,000 vessels a year, many of them sail-powered colliers carrying coal to ports around the world to refuel the new passenger carrying steamships.

Much of the town centre was built at the time the harbour was developed in the 1840s and today the mixture of small shops and businesses in its little-changed main thoroughfare, Queen Street, gives Amble a lively, bustling atmosphere.

Behind Queen Street lies the harbour, with parking available off Leazes Street near the RNLI station. On the quays here, catches are landed by the Amble fishing fleet - now the largest north of the Tyne - and fresh fish is available from a harbour-side shop.

For details of cruises to Coquet Island see page 46.

Up-river from the busy boatyard - where for more than a century many of the coast's traditional fishing cobles were built - is a 200 berth marina for yachts and motor cruisers opened in 1987. This, along with recent landscape and environmental improvements, has done much to enhance the appeal of the town known as "The Friendliest Port."

A Tourist Information Office in Dilston Terrace is open from Monday to Saturday between Easter and October, and for limited hours on Sundays in July and August.

The road from Amble to Warkworth passes the entrance to the Marina and parking and picnic areas near the Coquet Yacht Club and Amble Boat Club.

The Coquet estuary at Amble

Warkworth Castle

1 ¹/₂ miles north of Amble is

WARKWORTH

One of the prettiest villages in Northumberland, Warkworth's strategic importance as a crossing point on the River Coquet was recognised in medieval times.

The 14th century bridge which still spans the river carried traffic for 600 years and before the new road bridge was opened in 1965, the narrow arch of the sturdy gate tower proved a tight squeeze for large vehicles.

Warkworth Castle's mighty keep towers majestically above the village and its dramatic outline dominates the view from miles around.

A stronghold was first built on this commanding site above the Coquet's banks in the 12th century, although much of the fortifications seen today date from the 14th century when Warkworth came into the hands of the Percy family.

The riverside at Warkworth.

As the family's power and influence grew Warkworth Castle became their favourite residence and Harry Hotspur, the son of the 1st Earl of Northumberland, was brought up here.

At the age of 12 this precocious soldier was already fighting the Scots, leading the final assault against the defenders of besieged Berwick when its walls were breached.

Harry fell at the Battle of Shrewsbury in 1403, aged 37,and his feats were later immortalised by Shakespeare.

In the Bard's time, the great power of the Percies had declined and the castle allowed to fall into decay. Setting three scenes in his play, Henry IV, Part 1, at Warkworth, Shakespeare accurately described the castle as "this worm-eaten hold of ragged stone".

Now in the care of English Heritage, the castle is open 10am-6pm from April to November 1, and 10am-4pm in winter months.

Stone built houses and cottages, dating mainly from the 18th and 19th centuries, winding lanes and an abundance of colourful gardens all add to Warkworth's charm.

Castle Street slopes steeply down to Dial Place, the old market square, which is dominated by the Norman church of St. Lawrence.

This fine church was built in about 1200 following a devastating raid led by William the Lion in 1174 when the town was burnt to the ground and 300 women and children who had taken refuge in the 7th century Saxon church on this site were put to death.

The upper stage of the clock tower was added in the 14th century and its stone spire is one of only two dating back to medieval times to be found in Northumberland.

The church of St Lawrence at Warkworth, whose stone spire is one of only two in the county dating back to medieval times.

A unique historic site to be found on the wooded north bank of the river one mile west of the village, is Warkworth Hermitage. Open April 1 to September 30, on Wednesdays, Sundays & Bank Holidays (See walks page 55)

Dating from the 14th century, a flight of stone steps lead up to three chambers hewn out of the sandstone cliff, including a tiny chapel measuring 20 feet by 7 feet.

Described as the finest hermitage of its kind in the country, its creator is unknown.

A narrow road just north of the river bridge leads to a small car park and Warkworth beach.

(See beach guide page 56)

4¹/₂ miles north of Warkworth is

ALNMOUTH

Enjoying a picturesque setting on a headland on the north bank of the Aln estuary, Alnmouth can lay claim to the title of Northumberland's oldest port with a Royal charter bestowed by King John in 1207.

The view of Alnmouth from Church Hill, across the mouth of the River Aln.

Prosperous in the Middle Ages when its main exports were wool, hides and fish, it suffered much damage in 1336 when the Scots attacked from the sea and burned the town down.

Originally known as Alemouth, its importance as a corn port grew in the mid 18th century when a turnpike road gave the port a direct link to the fertile Tyne valley.

Many houses date from this period including several three storey buildings which were formerly granaries.

During this era, the coast was plagued by pirates. Two brigs loaded with valuable cargoes were seized off Alnmouth by French privateers in 1744 and in 1778 the infamous American pirate, Paul Jones, captured a vessel outside the port then, as a cheeky farewell gesture, fired a cannon shot at the town.

With the advent of railways, the corn trade dwindled and Alnmouth developed as an inshore fishing port with the new steam trains carrying catches to distant cities.

Spared from the noise of through traffic, the town's attractive Northumberland Street is rarely congested, and a large area for parking is available on the links at the north end of the bay. (See beach guide page 56)

Alnmouth Village Golf Club, established in 1869, is the second oldest links course in the country, and signs warn walkers " Danger flying golf balls".

Riverside Road overlooks the shallow, sandy estuary offering sheltered moorings for small boats and faces a grassy mound on the south side of the river, topped by a wooden cross.

Fishing cobles above the beach at Boulmer, where offshore reefs provide a natural shelter.

9

This is the site of a Saxon church dedicated to St. Waleric. The ruins of a chapel built here in 1154 by William de Vesci were blown down during a ferocious storm on Christmas Day 1806, when the flood-swollen river, which until then flowed south of Church Hill, burst through the low lying sand dunes and cut off this historic site from the rest of the village.

3 miles north of Alnmouth is

BOULMER

Sometimes by-passed by visitors touring the coast, this tiny fishing community is worth a special detour.

Thanks to the shelter offshore reefs give Boulmer Haven, no harbour was ever built here and the gently sloping beach allows fishing cobles to be hauled ashore with the help of a veteran collection of tractors which stand on the foreshore.

Once supporting 32 fishing families, most with the surnames Stanton or Stephenson, and used as an anchorage for roving Scottish herring boats, today only five cobles put to sea from Boulmer for crab, lobster and salmon.

Formerly a notorious smuggling village, today Boulmer is a peaceful spot that attracts many naturalists and beachcombers (See walks page 48).

Standing at the village's only road junction, St. Andrew's, which was built as a church and schoolroom by the Duke of Northumberland in 1881, vies for the title of smallest church on the coast.

Boulmer lost its RNLI lifeboat in 1968, but following intensive local fundraising a replacement boat was bought and fitted out and the independent Boulmer Volunteer Rescue Service was launched two years later.

1³/₄ miles from Boulmer, passing the RAF Air Sea Rescue helicopter base is

LONGHOUGHTON

Enlarged in modern times by new housing for families of servicemen based at nearby RAF Boulmer. Standing at the heart of the old village is the ancient Church of St. Peter and St. Paul. A few Saxon stonework features survived when the church was rebuilt in 1080 incorporating a strong square defensive tower with five feet thick walls which was used as a place of refuge during Scottish raids.

This ancient Parish Church was enlarged in the 12th century and carefully restored in 1874.

A road almost opposite the church, leads down to Low Steads Farm and the sea. (See beach guide page 59)

2 miles north is

HOWICK HALL

The manor of Howick has been in the hands of the Grey family since the 14th century.

A medieval tower which stood on the site of the present Hall was pulled down when this classical Georgian mansion was built in 1780. The Hall was altered in 1809 and rebuilt following a devastating fire in 1926.

In the Hall grounds, close to the roadside is the Church of St. Michael, built in 1849, which contains the tomb of the 2nd Earl Grey and his wife, Mary Elizabeth.

The gardens around Howick Hall contain a fine collection of trees, shrubs and herbaceous plants and the woodland garden is noted for its colourful displays of magnolias and rhododendrons. They are open to the public from April to October between 1pm and 6pm.

2³/4 miles from Howick Hall, via Howick Sea Houses farm, Howick hamlet and the 120 feet high cliffs at Cullernose Point, is

CRASTER

As the village closest to Dunstanburgh Castle, Craster attracts many visitors. A large car park is sited in an old quarry area behind the Tourist Information Centre, which stands at the entrance to the Arnold Memorial Nature Reserve managed by the Northumberland Wildlife Trust.

The harbour seen today was built by the Craster family in 1906 and until the 1940s was used to load coasters with locally quarried, hard-wearing whinstone carried to London for roadmaking. Craster's other famous export - the kipper- continues to flourish.

The famous Craster kippers were once produced from four curing yards in the village, but today only one, L.Robson & Sons, survives. Established in 1906, the firm occupies premises on Haven Hill which have been in continuous use since 1856.

Craster harbour.

Tours of the premises offer the chance to see the smoke houses that contain up to 2,500 brined herring which are smoked for 10 to 14 hours over fires of whitewood chippings covered with a layer of slow smouldering oak sawdust.

Following the demise of the local herring fishery Robson's now cure herring brought from Iceland and smoke Scottish salmon.

In the fishing boom days of the mid 19th century up to 50 boats operated from Craster, but today only a handful remain.

A short distance inland from the village is the 15th century Craster Tower, the family seat of the Craster family whose links with the area date back 800 years.

The Tourist Information Office is open daily between Easter and the end of October.

This aerial view illustrates the dramatic setting of Dunstanburgh – once the largest castle in Northumberland.

A one mile walk north of Craster leads to

Dunstanburgh Castle

Once the largest castle in Northumberland covering an 11 acre site, with six feet thick defensive walls and imposing 80 feet high towers, the dramatic ruins of Dunstanburgh were painted three times by Turner.

Protected by the 100 feet cliffs of Gull Crag to the north, a great defensive ditch 80 feet wide and 13 feet deep to the west, and the sea to the east, work on this massive stronghold was started in 1313 by Thomas, Earl of Lancaster, then the richest man in England apart from the King.

The power-hungry Earl was beheaded 9 years later for his traitorous dealings with the Scots, the castle became Crown property and in about 1325, Sir John Lilburn, the Constable of Dunstanburgh, added the imposing north west tower.

The castle was enlarged and strengthened later in the 14th century by John of Gaunt who wished to match the powerful fortresses of his rivals, the Percies, at Alnwick and Warkworth.

During the Wars of the Roses - when this Lancastrian stronghold changed hands five times - damage inflicted by cannon fire seriously weakened its fortifications and by Tudor times it was little more than a ruin.

Now, under the control of English Heritage, the castle is open daily between April 1 and November 1 10am – 6pm, and from Wednesday to Sunday 10am – 4pm between November and March. (See walk page 49)

2³/₄ miles from Craster is

EMBLETON

This quiet village lies ²/₃ of a mile from the sea which can be reached along a road leading to Dunstanburgh Castle Golf Course where footpaths cross the links to a large sandy bay. (See beach guide page 56-57)

Holy Trinity Church at Embleton has links with both the Craster and Grey families.

Embleton's Holy Trinity Parish Church has links with the area's two leading families, the Crasters and the Greys.

Built around 1200 and extensively rebuilt between 1330 and 1340, the church has a Grey Gallery which contains a memorial to Edward, 3rd Viscount Grey, Foreign Secretary during the First World War, and a porch commemorating members of the Craster family. Close to the church is a fortified Vicar's Pele Tower built in 1395 and converted into a house by eminent Northern architect John Dobson in 1828.

2 miles from Embleton is

NEWTON-BY-THE-SEA

A right turn at the junction of the B1339 and B1340 leads to High Newton and on down to Low Newton, a little fishing village with a history dating back 700 years.

Close to the seashore is a grassy square enclosed on three sides by white painted fishermen's cottages, now in the ownership of the National Trust.

Horse riders on the beach in front of the square at Low Newton

This sheltered bay is popular with water sports enthusiasts and walkers and behind dunes to the south of the square is the Newton Pool Nature Reserve. (See walks page 50)

5 miles from Low Newton is

BEADNELL

While the ruins of a seafront chapel at Ebb's Nook date back to the 1200s and there are records of fishing tithes being paid to monks in the 14th century, Beadnell developed on its inland site around the 16th century pele tower which now forms part of the The Craster Arms.

In the early 1700s the village consisted of two rows of cottages, several granaries - one of which is now the Beadnell Towers Hotel - and a few large mansions including the late 17th century Beadnell Hall.

St. Ebba's Church which stands in the centre of the village was built in 1746.

Sunset at Beadnell, the east coast harbour with a west facing entrance.

A road from the village leads down to the seafront and along past old wooden fishermen's huts perched above rocky inlets to the harbour at the north end of Beadnell Bay, which was built in 1796. Work began three years later on the impressive limekilns which produced lime for agricultural use.

The growing importance of herring fishing led in 1822 to the limekilns being converted into fish curing houses and herring yards were built nearby in 1827.

The harbour, which is said to be the only port on the east coast of England with a west facing entrance, was given to local fishermen by J.M.Craster in 1949.

In its heyday, this was the home base for 20 herring keel boats but now only three small boats keep the centuries old Beadnell fishing tradition alive.

The sheltered waters of Beadnell Bay are a favourite with sailing and water sports enthusiasts, and a large pay car park is located immediately behind the beach near Beadnell caravan site.

(See beach guide page 57)

CHAPTER TWO

FISHING HERITAGE

Families living in the small communities scattered along the sparsely populated north Northumberland coast have wrested a precarious living from the sea for more than 700 years.

But as the 19th century began, the need to supply fresh food to the expanding populations of Britain's industrial cities saw the rapid growth of this traditional occupation into a major industry.

The inshore waters off Northumberland were rich in white fish and shellfish and an increasing number of sail driven small fishing boats - known as cobles and mules - were soon fishing out of Berwick, Spittal, Boulmer, Newton-by-the-Sea and Alnmouth.

Other harbours had growing fleets of wooden, 2-masted herring keel boats; 20 at Beadnell, 25 at Holy Island and 33 at tiny Craster.

While records for 1856 show that the busiest fishing port along this coastline was North Sunderland/Seahouses which supported 51 local herring boats.

When the giant shoals of herring moved into inshore waters during the summer months, fishing boats from Scotland, Cornwall and the Isle of Man joined forces with the local fishing fleets.

Handling the vast quantities of fish landed at East Coast ports was an itinerant band of " herrin' lasses " - including women from Northumberland fishing families - who followed the roving herring fleets as they worked their way south from the Scottish isles to Yarmouth.

It is said that these tough, hard working women could single-handedly split, gut and pack several thousand herring a day. Each barrel would hold up to 800 fish and their pay was one shilling a barrel!

Herring Keel boats in Seahouses harbour.

And it is claimed that a 3 strong crew of Seahouses women held the record for productivity, managing to pack an astonishing 24 barrels in a single day!

Prior to the development of smoking as a preservative, salted herring - known locally as winter beef - was packed in barrels destined for all parts of England, ports in Germany and Russia, and even the slave colonies of America.

It was also in Seahouses that a roving fish merchant, an "Englishman" from south of Northumberland named John Woodger, invented the kipper in 1843 after conducting various smoking trials in the yard of what is today The Olde Ship Hotel.

Previously whole herring had been smoked to make "bloaters" but the new technique using split herring and a curing process that involved overnight smoking produced a tasty end product that remained edible for at least one week.

The 1840s and 50s were boom days for the Northumberland fishing ports but when a major inquiry was held into the inshore fishing industry in 1863, the first signs of trouble were beginning to show.

Local fishermen complained of unfair competition as a result of overfishing by French boats, who, unlike the God-fearing Northumberland men who rested on the Sabbath, actually fished 7 days a week. Catches, they claimed, were becoming smaller and prices were falling.

Yet North Sunderland harbour was becoming increasingly busy and, in the 1880s, it was substantially enlarged.

At the peak of the herring fishing season in the boom years between 1895 and 1910, it was common for up to 300 boats - many from Scotland, France and Holland - to land fish at Seahouses every day and this massive supply kept 10 herring yards at full stretch.

In the face of outside competition, the local fishing families gradually switched to ever larger vessels, in some cases almost twice the size of the old keel boats. The new herring boats required more men to crew them and as a result, the numerical size of the locally based herring fleets fell. By the end of the century, the Seahouses fleet had reduced to only 19 herring keel boats and Beadnell's herring fleet had shrunk to 10 boats.

The herring remained plentiful but gradually as the specialist Scottish and foreign herring fleets began using more advanced, and more deadly, fishing methods requiring ever larger, more costly vessels, the investment required became too great for many Northumberland fishermen whose herring fishing season only lasted from June to September.

In early autumn their small 2-masted herring keel boats were hauled ashore and the 8-10 man crews took to their smaller fishing boats for autumn lobster fishing, then winter long-line fishing for cod, haddock and plaice.

These long lines carried 1200 hooks or more and each hook had to be hand- baited with mussels, limpets or lugworm.

A forest of masts: the herring fleet at anchor.

Veteran Seahouses fisherman, Andrew Rutter, can still recall the long hours fishermen's wives uncomplainingly spent baiting lines.

Each fisherman had three "half" lines with the carefully spaced hooks tied to the strong hand-made hemp line with thin cotton sneeds. While two half lines were being fished, his wife would start work at 5.00 in the morning prising open hundreds of mussel shells before starting to bait the spare half line.

On her husband's return from the sea, a second line had to be untangled and baited in the afternoon, and if the tide prevented the menfolk coming ashore in time, it was the women who went onto the rocks to gather the next day's bait.

There was surely widespread relief in all the fishing families when the spring crabbing and lobster fishing began and by late May the herring boats were painted, overhauled and made ready for sea again.

But as the old sail powered keel boats were superseded by larger steam powered vessels, for many of the coast's old fishing families - Dawson, Dixon, Douglas, Fawcus, Hall, Robson, Rutter, Shiel, Stanton, Stephenson - herring fishing came to an end.

Beadnell's last herring boat was laid up in 1914 and at Seahouses, the last keel boat, the Speedwell, owned by the Dawson family, survived until the 1920s.

Small dual purpose boats which could be used for seine net fishing as well as the seasonal crab and lobster fishing were introduced and the traditional cobles were soon enjoying the benefits of engine power.

After the 1939-45 war a brief boom was again enjoyed by the local boats but with the introduction by national fishing fleets of large purse nets and otter trawls, which scoured previously untouched areas of the seabed, fish stocks dramatically fell.

Today, with numerous bureaucratic restrictions, catch quotas and competition from cheap foreign imports, north Northumberland's remaining inshore fishermen are fighting for survival.

A fleet of boats still lands whitefish and shellfish at Amble. Scampi is the main catch of the handful of large boats still operating from Seahouses, and crab and lobster are the mainstay of the cobles and other small fishing boats at Beadnell, Boulmer, Holy Island, Craster, Tweedmouth, Alnmouth and Newton-by-the-Sea.

Many of these fishermen only manage to earn a living wage by continuing the centuries-old tradition of net fishing for salmon off the coast.

The 60 salmon boat licences issued between the Tweed and the Tyne have in the past been handed down from one generation to the next or sold on to another fishing family. Now this practice is to be stopped and within a decade that is likely to bring all salmon net fishing to an end.

A fascinating insight into the lives of these traditional fisherfolk, the hardships they endured, the dangers they faced, and the vital support role played by the fishermen's wives, is graphically illustrated at the Marine Life & Fishing Heritage Centre near Seahouses harbour.

CHAPTER THREE

COASTAL DRIVE

Starting in Seahouses and travelling north up the coastline through Bamburgh and Waren Mill on to the border town of Berwick.

2 miles from Beadnell is

SEAHOUSES

Once the busiest fishing harbour on the coast, today the brightly painted boats which carry 35,000 visitors a year to the Farne Islands far outnumber those still engaged in fishing.

When Seahouses consisted of only a few fishermen's cottages, North Sunderland, half a mile inland, was a substantial township and today it still gives its name to the harbour and the RNLI lifeboat station.

A short pier built here in the late 1700s was used for loading lime from the large seafront kilns but by the time this trade ceased in the 1860s, Seahouses had become a major fishing centre with a home fleet of more than 60 boats.

As the East Coast herring fleet grew ever larger, the harbour was enlarged in the 1880s to cope with as many as 300 boats lining up to discharge their catches every day at the height of the season.

The opening of the main East Coast railway meant that the fish landed at Seahouses could reach the major cities of England in record time - even though it had to be carried 5 miles to the nearest station at Chathill by horse and cart.

However, in 1898 a single track line operated by the North Sunderland Railway was opened between Seahouses and Chathill and this narrow gauge steam train which pulled three passenger carriages at little more than walking speed was a big favourite with holidaymakers until its closure in 1951.

Trips from Seahouses to the Farne Islands, once a sideline for the local fishermen, have now become a well organised tourist service operated in conjunction with the National Trust, whose prime concern is to balance the large number of visitors wishing to see the islands with the need to protect seabird breeding colonies from unnecessary disturbance.

From April until the end of September, landings are permitted on Inner Farne and Staple Island, and in October cruises around the Farne Islands without a landing are available.

The National Trust charges landing fees of £4.00 per person in May, June and July, and £3-00 in April, August and September.

(See Farne Islands page 42)

One of the most popular attractions in Seahouses is the wide variety of cafes, restaurants, and pubs offering the chance to sample excellent fish and chips or fresh crab sandwiches.

An aerial view of Seahouses.

Inner Farne (background) is a summer destination for boat trips from Seahouses.

Of the ten herring yards and smokehouses that operated in the town during the last century, only one, run by John Swallow above the harbour in South Street, is still in business.

Next to the smokehouse, in the Fisherman's Kitchen shop, (open from 9am daily, Monday to Saturday) photographs portraying the fishermen and boats of yesteryear are displayed together with a collection of tools used to make the old wooden herring barrels.

Places worth a visit include the RNLI Lifeboat Station, the Marine Life and Fishing Heritage Centre (open 10am daily, April to October), and the Olde Ship Hotel, where landlord Alan Glen has filled the busy bar overlooking the harbour with a superb collection of fishing memorabilia.

A tourist information centre can be found at the entrance to the large pay car park located behind the main street.

It is open daily from 10am between Easter and October. Parking for a £1 charge is also available on the hill near the RNLI station and on the main pier.

The National Trust shop is open daily from 10am between April and October.

3 miles from Seahouses is

BAMBURGH

Once the capital of the Royal Kingdom of Northumbria, this small, picturesque village attracts visitors from all over the world.

The first stronghold sited on the black rocky outcrop where Bamburgh Castle stands today was a timber fortress built in 547 by Ida the Flamebearer who ruled the land between the Forth and the Tyne known as Bernicia.

In 604, Ida's grandson, Ethelfrith the Destroyer, extended the kingdom to the Humber creating Northumbria and after giving this royal fortress to his wife Bebba, it became known as Bebban burgh and then Bamburgh.

Throughout the 7th century, spanning the reigns of Edwin, Oswald, Oswi and Ecgfrith, Bamburgh and nearby Lindisfarne were at the heart of a kingdom which nurtured the birth of English christianity and were renowned centres of culture, art and scholarship.

Bamburgh remained a royal capital serving 30 Saxon kings until the death of Eric Bloodaxe, the last king of Northumbria, in 954.

Bamburgh Castle

The first stone built castle at Bamburgh was constructed by Henry II in the late 12th century. Badly damaged by the Scots in 1297 it was rebuilt and thought to be impregnable until 1464. Defended by followers of Henry VI it was besieged by Edward IV's army and became the first English castle to fall as a result of artillery fire.

The 16th century saw the powerful Forster family installed at the castle but as their fortunes declined in the following century, the castle fell into neglect and, when bought in 1704 by Lord Crewe, the last Prince Bishop of Durham, it was in a ruinous state.

Following the Bishop's death in 1722, the castle was left to a charitable trust, and in the capable hands of trustee, Dr John Sharp, the Archdeacon of Northumberland, restoration began and the castle was used to accommodate a charity school for girls, a dispensary for the poor, and an infirmary for shipwrecked mariners. (See page 61).

In 1894 the castle was bought for £60,000 by Lord Armstrong, the Tyneside gunmaker and engineer, and over the next 10 years the wealthy industrialist spent £1m on rebuilding and restoration.

Today, the castle remains in the ownership of his descendants and is open to visitors between Easter and October from 11am to 5pm daily.

The 800 year old Norman keep and other public rooms contain fine exhibits of arms and armour, porcelain, jade, china and furniture from many periods.

From the castle ramparts there are spectacular views of Holy Island and the Farne Islands and this picturesque setting has featured in several major films including Becket and Macbeth.

———————

Bamburgh's other magnet for visitors is the RNLI's museum dedicated to the village's famous heroine, Grace Darling. Standing a few doors from the cottage where Grace was born in 1815, the museum contains paintings, memorabilia and dramatic contemporary accounts of the sea rescue in which Grace and her lighthouse keeper father saved the lives of 9 people after the sinking of the paddle steamer Forfarshire in 1838. (See page 63)

The museum is open from Easter to September 30 from 11am to 6pm.

A canopied monument to Grace, who died from TB aged only 26, can be found opposite the museum in St. Aidan's Churchyard and nearby is a monument to Dr Sharp, the man who pioneered many schemes to help prevent loss of life at sea.

Built on the site of a wooden church where St. Aidan died in 651, the pink sandstone church is architecturally one of the finest in the county.

The large nave with two arcades of four arches dates from about 1200. Completed later in the 13th century was the square tower and a vaulted crypt below the chancel - discovered during alterations in 1837- where it is believed relics associated with St. Aidan were once held. (See walk page 51) (See beach guide page 58)

An aerial view of Bamburgh Castle, with the village in the foreground.

2¹/₂ miles from Bamburgh is

WAREN MILL

In the 13th century, when Berwick was still part of Scotland, Warenmouth on the southern shore of Budle Bay was the most northerly port in England.

Later known as Newtown, the importance of this once busy grain port declined after Berwick passed permanently into English hands in 1482 and the harbour gradually fell into disuse.

The 18th century mill on the roadside at the head of the bay occupies a site where mills have stood since 1187. Ships which brought corn to feed the mill and carried away cargoes of flour revived the harbour's fortunes during the 19th century but the last grain ship to enter the port was recorded in December 1881.

The old quay in Budle Bay.

The old quay still standing on the south shore of Budle Bay was rebuilt in about 1912 to handle cargoes of whinstone from Kittling Hill quarry but this trade ended after only a few years.

Today the only arrivals and departures are the many waterfowl - including brent and greylag geese, redshank, widgeon and ringed and grey plover - who find sanctuary and a plentiful supply of food in this shallow, sheltered bay. (See walk page 51)

LINDISFARNE NATIONAL NATURE RESERVE

Established in 1964, this 8650 acre reserve stretches from Budle Bay north to Cheswick Black Rocks encompassing most of the shoreline of Holy Island and some of the finest dunes, saltmarshes and mudflats in Britain.

Due to the vast number of ducks, wildfowl and waders that visit the area - particularly in winter - it has been designated a "wetland of international importance".

Access to the reserve is unrestricted but visitors' attention is drawn to warning notices about unexploded ordnance, quicksands at Goswick and Cheswick and soft mud at Fenham Flats.

From Waren Mill follow the signposted Coastal Route which leads inland towards Belford and on to the A1 for Berwick.

Between this junction and the Beal junction - for access to Holy Island - several minor roads are signposted leading down to a quiet stretch of coastline largely consisting of areas of salt marsh and mud flats.

At **Fenham-le-Moor**, 1$1/4$ miles off the Al, the road ends at the shoreline where there is a limited amount of parking space a short distance from a wildlife observation hide.

A further 2 miles north up the A1, a road leads to **Fenham Mill** where limited roadside parking is possible before reaching the road end. A footpath leads down onto the shoreline which overlooks Fenham Flats and Holy Island - an excellent observation point for birdwatchers.

At quiet Goswick Sands the tide retreats a mile at low water.

Continuing north up the A1, past the road leading to Holy Island causeway and 2 miles beyond Haggerston Castle and Caravan Park, a road leads to Cheswick and Berwick Golf Club and along a poorly surfaced road to Beachcomber House holiday cottages and camp site and **Goswick Sands.**

A shoreline footpath here travels 2 miles south to Beal Causeway and the campsite owners offer permissive access down onto the sweeping flat sands where the tide recedes almost one mile at low water. A cafe and bar here are open in season to non-residents.

Rejoining the A1 continue north to a roundabout and the A1167 to Berwick.

For access to **Cocklawburn** beach turn into Scremerston and follow the signposted road for 1½ miles to a stretch of rocky coastline with small sandy bays that offers views south to Holy Island and Bamburgh.

Spittal promenade

After 1¹/₂ miles follow signs to

Spittal

Once a busy fishing village and a popular spa resort in Victorian times, Spittal's name is derived from the siting of a leper hospital here in medieval times.

Behind the long, wide main street lined with sturdy 18th and 19th century stone houses is a pleasant promenade bordering a long sandy beach.

Continue along the coast road to

Tweedmouth

Bought by the Corporation of Berwick, along with Spittal, for a mere £570 in 1657, Tweedmouth was until the 15th century a tiny fishing village lying in the shadow of what was the Scottish-held seaport of Berwick.

Travel along past the RNLI lifeboat station near the tiny quay at Carr Rock and the award-winning Rob Roy seafood restaurant, on a road that offers fine sea level views across the Tweed estuary to Berwick.

The main street leads onto the Old Border Bridge which crosses into Berwick.

The Old Border Bridge has spanned the Tweed for nearly 500 years.

The massive Elizabethan town walls are considered the best surviving example in Europe.

BERWICK

A Royal Burgh when Glasgow was only a village, Berwick grew to be the largest and most prosperous town in Scotland during the 13th century.

Between 1296 and 1482 fighting between the English and Scots meant that it changed hands no fewer than 10 times. Although it remained under English control throughout the 16th century, it was regarded as an occupied stronghold on foreign soil until the Union of Crowns in 1603, and it was not until 1836 that Berwick legally became part of England.

The most impressive legacy of Berwick's former strategic importance as a front-line military stronghold are the massive Elizabethan walls built between 1558 and 1570 to defend the town from both land and sea attack by the Scots or their French allies.

These famous fortifications, which replaced earlier medieval defences, are considered the best surviving example of a defensive town wall in Europe.

Following the Union between England and Scotland, peace and prosperity gradually returned to Berwick and this once isolated town gradually began to restore its trading links with the outside world.

In 1611 work began on a stone bridge across the Tweed to replace an old wooden Tudor structure. Now known as the Old Border Bridge, this 15 arched road bridge which carried all traffic using the Great North Road until the opening of the Royal Tweed Bridge in 1928, still provides a local link between Tweedmouth and Berwick.

During the 18th century Berwick's importance as a port rapidly grew. In 1793 records reveal that barley, corn, eggs and salmon accounted for much of its trade.

And in that year, the importance of the local fishing industry is shown by the statistic that 28,100 barrels of pickled herring were shipped from the port.

During the 19th century two major developments changed the face of the estuary. A $^1/_2$ mile long pier on the north side of the river was completed in 1821, and the 28 arched Royal Border Bridge, designed by Robert Stephenson, was built across the Tweed. Its opening in 1850 completed the first continuous East Coast railway link between London and Edinburgh.

Today this most northerly of all English towns, which lies 3 miles south of the border, still exudes a strong Scottish flavour through the accents of its townspeople, the presence of Scottish banks and banknotes and the local football club's membership of the Scottish Football League.

The large Castle Gate car park, next to the Tourist Information Office (open daily between Easter and September, and from Monday to Saturday between October and March), is a good starting point for a walk around the old town walls.

"Exploring Berwick" leaflets produced by Berwick Civic Society which offer a choice of walks around the town can be obtained here.

Among the many places of interest worth a visit are the Berwick Barracks dating from 1721. Here there is the regimental museum of the King's Own Scottish Borderers - one of the best military museums in the country - plus a permanent English Heritage exhibition "By Beat of Drum" following the history of infantry soldiers from Elizabethan days to modern times, and the Borough Museum and Art Gallery.

(The Barracks museum and exhibition is open daily from 10am between April and October, and from Wednesday to Sunday between November and March. The Borough Museum and Art Gallery is open from 10am daily, April to September, and from Wednesday to Sunday during winter.)

Holy Trinity Church built in 1652 in The Parade was one of only two churches built during Oliver Cromwell's reign as Lord Protector of the Commonwealth. In its original Puritan design it had no altar, steeple or bells.

The Wine and Spirit Museum in Palace Green offers a fascinating insight into the secrets of distilling and smuggling. (Open Mon- Sat 9am to 5pm, and Sundays 12 noon - 4.30pm.)

A view over Berwick looking south.

Much of the town's best architecture dates from the 18th and 19th centuries, with many finely restored properties to be seen in Quay Walls and Ravensdowne.

Marygate, where a street market is held twice weekly on Wednesdays and Saturdays, is dominated by the Town Hall built in the 1750s as a civic meeting place and the town gaol. (There are guided tours of the third floor Cell Block Museum at 10.30am and 2pm from Monday to Friday between Easter and September.)

Berwick has been noted for its salmon fishery since the 12th century and a limited number of boats are still permitted to carry on the traditional net fishing for salmon in the River Tweed between mid February and mid September.

Another export for which Berwick is famous, that renowned sweet, the Berwick Cockle, was first made in 1801 at 64-66 Bridge Street, one of the town's oldest thoroughfares. The Cowe family has continued the business on the same premises since 1886.

CHAPTER FOUR

THE ISLANDS OF NORTH NORTHUMBERLAND

Lindisfarne Castle once housed a small royal garrison.

THE HOLY ISLAND OF LINDISFARNE

When King Oswald asked the monks of Iona to help establish christianity in Northumbria in 635, the man given the task, Aidan, chose this place to build the first primitive wooden, thatch-roofed church and monastery in the heathen kingdom.

From this humble beginning Lindisfarne was to became the centre of christianity in Saxon England for the next two and a half centuries.

Of the 16 men who served as Bishops of Lindisfarne over the following 240 years, the most illustrious was Cuthbert. Appointed prior in 665, this saintly missionary who worked tirelessly to convert Northumbrians to christianity found solitude by retreating to the rocky islet lying close to the island's west shore, now known as St.Cuthbert's Isle.

As his fame grew and large numbers of pilgrims descended on Lindisfarne, the exhausted Cuthbert retreated in 676 to a hermit's cell on Inner Farne, remaining there for 9 years until he was persuaded to accept the bishopric.

Within two years, worn out by his labours, he returned to the peace and solitude of his Farne sanctuary where he died in 687.

Established by this time as a centre for scholarship and creativity, the famous Lindisfarne Gospels were produced here by Bishop Eadfrith in about 698.

The Golden Age of Lindisfarne ended in 875, when its monks were forced to flee Danish raiders taking with them the Gospels together with Cuthbert's remains and the bones of St. Aidan.

A small band of Benedictine monks returned to the island in the late 11th century and between 1090 and 1140 they built the magnificent priory whose picturesque red sandstone ruins remain today.

The celebrated book of Gospels, comprising 258 leaves of parchment and 22,800 lines of script, was returned to Lindisfarne in the 12th century where it remained for 400 years, before being bought privately and finally given to the British Museum.

An English Heritage museum outside the priory grounds is open from 10am daily throughout the year.

Following the Dissolution of Monasteries by Henry Vlll in 1537 monastic life on the island came to an end, and large sections of the priory were pulled down to provide stone for a fort in the south east corner of the island on Beblowe Crag which was completed in 1550.

Lindisfarne Castle

A small royal garrison remained on the island until 1819, and the castle was rescued from neglect and decay at the turn of the century when it was bought by the wealthy publisher Edward Hudson who commissioned architect, Sir Edwin Lutyens, to convert it into a luxurious private home.

Later bought by bankers, O.T.Falk and then Sir Edward de Stein, the castle was given to the National Trust in 1944.

It is open to visitors from April to October, daily except Fridays, for 4¹/₂ hours - subject to tides - between 10.30am and 4.30pm.

Open at the same hours is the small walled garden, designed by Gertrude Jekyll for her friend Lutyens, which is sited on a south facing slope 500 yards north of the castle.

It is said that when this very stout gardening guru first came to the island, it took four men to lift her out of the boat she arrived in.

When the garden was restored a few years ago by the National Trust many of the shrubs and perennials included in Miss Jekyll's original planting plan were used.

Standing close to Lindisfarne Priory is the Parish Church of St Mary where a copy of the Lindisfarne Gospels is displayed. The rock known as St. Cuthbert's Isle can be seen from the churchyard and by the entrance path is the petting stone which, by island tradition, new brides leap over for good luck.

Apart from its historic attractions, peace and quiet can be found on Holy Island by exploring its beautiful, unspoilt coastline.

The dunes are noted for wild orchids and the quiet shoreline attracts many species of breeding birds in summer and thousands of migratory birds in winter. (See walk page 53)

The harbour which now offers a sheltered anchorage for yachtsmen was a busy port in the last century serving the island's limestone and ironstone quarries, and the tarred upturned keels of the old herring boats near the harbour are a poignant reminder of days when the island had a 50 strong fishing fleet.

For an insight into the lives of the fishing families here in the last century, visit the Museum of Island Life at Hillcroft Cottage, (open daily from Easter to the end of October) which belonged to the Markwell family from the 1840s onwards. Among the many exhibits there is a fascinating collection of old photographs.

Visitors are reminded that the 3 mile causeway linking the island to the mainland is covered twice a day by the incoming tide. The safe crossing period is usually from $3^1/_2$ hours after high tide until about 2 hours before the next high water.

The atmospheric ruins of Lindisfarne priory.

Several motorists every year fail to heed the safe crossing notices displayed at either end of the causeway, lose their race with the incoming tide, and have to spend several uncomfortable hours in a refuge box unless rescued by lifeboatmen.

Before the causeway was built in 1954, visitors who travelled to Beal by train were brought across the sand flats by horse drawn traps and later by old Ford taxis.

The route taken by earlier visitors - the ancient Pilgrim's Way - is marked by a line of wooden poles cutting diagonally across the flats.

In winter this inter-tidal area attracts tens of thousands of waders and wildfowl.

Holy Island's sheltered anchorage.

THE FARNE ISLANDS

By arrangement with the National Trust visitors are allowed to land on Inner Farne and Staple Island between April and the end of September. (See page 24)

The Farne Islands lie between $1^1/2$ miles and $4^3/4$ miles offshore and are spread over a 7 square mile area consisting of 15 main islands and a further 13 exposed at low water.

Both Aidan and Cuthbert spent time on Inner Farne in lone meditation and prayer, a number of hermits followed in their footsteps and the island was permanently occupied by monks from the mid 13th century until 1536.

On small areas of thin soil on Inner Farne - which extends over 16 acres at low water - and on Staple and Brownsman Islands, they raised crops, reared cattle, and supplemented their food supplies with birds' eggs, fish and seals.

A surviving monument to these self-sufficient early islanders is the Chapel of St. Cuthbert built on Inner Farne in 1370 and restored in the 19th century. Nearby is the fortified tower which stood four storeys high when it was built by Thomas Castell, Prior of Durham, in the early 1500s.

Today it provides accommodation for the National Trust wardens who monitor and protect the seabird colonies during the spring and summer breeding season.

The tower is said to occupy the site where in 676 Cuthbert built a spartan windowless cell with an opening in the roof so that he was cut off from " the view of every object but heaven".

The first crude lighthouse on the island is recorded in 1673 when a coal fire was lit nightly on top of this stone tower.

In the 18th century a second tower was built on Staple Island and when this was destroyed in 1783 a replacement was built on Brownsman Island.

In 1809 a modern lighthouse with oil lights was built on Inner Farne followed a year later by a second on Brownsman. This proved an unsatisfactory site, and in 1826 it was replaced by the 85 feet tall Longstone Light which was completed in only ten months.

Its first keeper was William Darling who took up residence with his wife and 8 children including daughter Grace, then aged 11.

Twelve years later came the dramatic sea rescue that would make Grace world famous. (See page 63)

In 1922 the inner group of islands was put up for sale and thanks to the efforts of the Northumberland, Durham and Newcastle Natural History Societies, a public appeal was launched by Viscount Grey of Falloden to raise the purchase price.

Lord Armstrong, the owner of the outer group of islands, also agreed to sell them if the appeal was successful, and in 1925 all the islands were purchased and handed over to the National Trust.

Today the Farne Islands are a National Nature Reserve and a world famous wildlife sanctuary. In spring and early summer some 68,000 pairs of seabirds nest here including cormorant, four species of tern, eider duck, shag, kittiwake, herring gull, guillemot and puffin.

Many more summer bird migrants have been recorded as passing visitors, and in autumn thousands of winter residents begin to arrive including longtailed duck, red throated diver and grebe.

Puffins, often called sea parrots, are the most numerous nesting bird on the Farnes, with recent estimates showing some 34,000 pairs on Staple and Brownsman Islands and the West Wideopens where they lay their eggs in old rabbit burrows.

The tall rock stacks off Staple Island, known as the Pinnacles, are a favourite with guillemots while up to 1500 pairs of eider duck prefer Inner Farne or the North and South Wamses.

The critical nesting period for most species is between early May to late July and for that reason, visitors are restricted in these months to morning landings on Staple Island and afternoon landings on Inner Farne.

Above: an aerial view of the Farne Islands looking north east, Inner Farne in the foreground.

Left: puffins are the most numerous birds on the Farnes, with an estimated 34,000 nesting pairs.

Grey Seals

The Farnes colony of Atlantic grey seals is one of the most important in the world and the largest in England.

Records of their presence here date back 800 years and from medieval times until the last century they were valued for their rich body oil. One transaction by monks living on Inner Farne in the 14th century shows that they received 27 shillings for six seals.

Since 1932 the Farnes seals have been protected by Act of Parliament. As a result their numbers have dramatically increased - and they are often seen swimming in the choppy waters around the islands or basking on rocks.

Larger than the common seal, Atlantic grey bulls can weigh up to 600 lbs, measure 2.3 metres in length and, contrary to their name, have a coat that is dark brown in colour when dry, and appears black when wet.

The smaller cows have silvery-grey upper bodies with dark patches and usually calve in November. The main nursery islands are the North and South Wamses and the Northern Hares.

Atlantic grey seals basking on rocks in the Farnes.

They produce a single pup which is creamy white at birth and weighs about 30lbs.

Tagged Farne seals have been found as far away as Norway, Holland and Germany, and they are regular visitors off many beaches along the north Northumberland coast.

COQUET ISLAND

Although landings are not permitted on this island which lies 1 mile offshore, 1-hour boat trips run from Amble harbour between May and August. Sailing times are available from the town's Tourist Information Office.

Following in the footsteps of St. Cuthbert, who visited the island in 684, it was used over many centuries as a place of sanctuary by monks seeking solitude.

The 80 feet tall lighthouse was built in 1841, on the base of a fortified tower used by soldiers who garrisoned the island in the 17th century, and built into the lighthouse keeper's cottage are the remains of a chapel and priest's cell once used by hermit monks.

The practice of allowing day trippers to land on the island which led to bird numbers declining, was halted some years ago and in 1972 the island, which is owned by the Duke of Northumberland, became an RSPB protected reserve. A warden is now based on the island throughout the breeding season between March and September.

Some 20,000 pairs of seabirds now nest and hatch their young every year on the 14 acre island which is one of the last refuges in the United Kingdom for the endangered roseate tern.

Around 30 pairs of this rare bird have been counted among the 3,000 pairs of the more numerous Arctic, common and sandwich terns.

Thousands of puffins nest on the island which is also the most southerly breeding site on the East Coast of the eider duck, and other regular visitors include fulmars, black-headed gulls, oyster catchers, guillemots and kittiwakes.

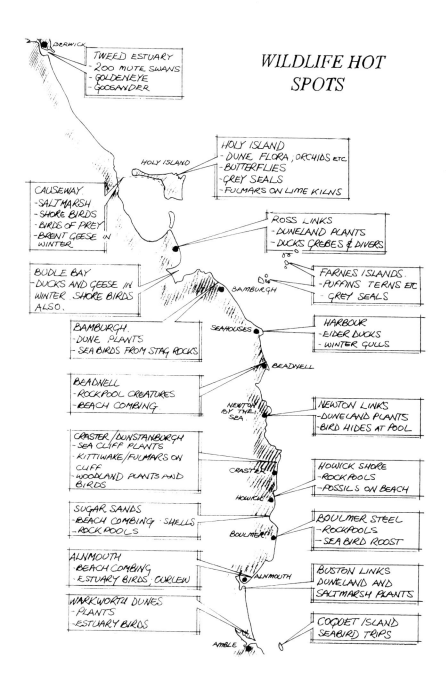

WILDLIFE HOT SPOTS

BERWICK

TWEED ESTUARY
- 200 MUTE SWANS
- GOLDENEYE
- GOOSANDER

HOLY ISLAND

HOLY ISLAND
- DUNE FLORA; ORCHIDS ETC
- BUTTERFLIES
- GREY SEALS
- FULMARS ON LIME KILNS

CAUSEWAY
- SALTMARSH
- SHORE BIRDS
- BIRDS OF PREY
- BRENT GEESE IN WINTER

ROSS LINKS
- DUNELAND PLANTS
- DUCKS GREBES & DIVERS

BUDLE BAY
- DUCKS AND GEESE IN WINTER. SHORE BIRDS ALSO.

BAMBURGH

FARNES ISLANDS.
- PUFFINS TERNS ETC
- GREY SEALS

BAMBURGH.
- DUNE PLANTS
- SEA BIRDS FROM STAG ROCKS

SEAHOUSES

HARBOUR
- EIDER DUCKS
- WINTER GULLS

BEADNELL

BEADNELL
- ROCKPOOL CREATURES
- BEACH COMBING

NEWTON BY THE SEA

NEWTON LINKS
- DUNELAND PLANTS
- BIRD HIDES AT POOL

CRASTER / DUNSTANBURGH
- SEA CLIFF PLANTS
- KITTIWAKE/FULMARS ON CLIFF
- WOODLAND PLANTS AND BIRDS

CRASTER

HOWICK

HOWICK SHORE
- ROCKPOOLS
- FOSSILS ON BEACH

SUGAR SANDS
- BEACH COMBING · SHELLS
- ROCK POOLS

BOULMER

BOULMER STEEL
- ROCKPOOLS
- SEA BIRD ROOST

ALNMOUTH
- BEACH COMBING
- ESTUARY BIRDS · CURLEW

ALNMOUTH

BUSTON LINKS
DUNELAND AND SALTMARSH PLANTS

WARKWORTH DUNES
- PLANTS
- ESTUARY BIRDS

COQUET ISLAND
SEABIRD TRIPS

AMBLE

CHAPTER FIVE

WALKS

BOULMER HAVEN (1 on map, Back Page)

Two long offshore rocky spurs known as North and South Reins give Boulmer Haven some protection from the turbulent force of the North Sea and provide local fishermen with a safe anchorage.

And the sheltered beach is a favourite feeding area in autumn and winter for a large variety of birds including plover, redshank, curlew, dunlin, bar-tailed godwit, cormorant and eider duck.

Park on the green overlooking the Haven and set off southwards along the links towards the red and white navigation posts, which help boats line up a safe passage through the narrow gap between the offshore rocks.

Boulmer Haven from the south.

A small promontory ahead offers views south to Coquet Island and north to Dunstanburgh Castle. Drop down to the shoreline where, at low tide, rockpools and seaweed beds are well worth exploring.

Follow the shoreline northwards beyond the fishermen's cottages. Just before the shelving rocks are reached, climb the narrow path that leads steeply up the bank away from the shore and joins a bridle path where you can either return to the village or continue northwards to Boulmer Steel and on into Howdiemont Bay and Sugar Sands. (See beach guide page 59)

CRASTER- DUNSTANBURGH (5 on map)

The most popular route to Dunstanburgh Castle follows the shoreline but on a wet or windy day the following walk offers a more sheltered path to this historic landmark.

From the Information Centre car park, cross the road and go through a wicket gate marked by a National Trust sign to Dunstanburgh Heughs.

After passing through an old wooded quarry area, the path leads through a second gate and joins a wider track that travels along below the inland edge of the Heugh, the last mainland stretch of the Great Whin Sill which re-emerges several miles to the north to form the Farne Islands.

Continue on until reaching another wicket gate in a field fence. Turn right on to a farm track which climbs the Heugh to provide a splendid view of ruined Dunstanburgh.

Turn right through the first of two adjacent field gates, and follow the fence line for 100 yards. Turn left through the next gate and follow the fence line down to join the shoreline path that leads to the castle.

Historic Dunstanburgh Castle.

49

After passing through two gates, the path reaches a small bay where Henry VIII's fleet anchored in 1514.

Beyond the next gate bear right along the shoreline on a path leading to Queen Margaret's Cove, also known as Rumble Churn, a deep narrow inlet which at high tide is filled with the roar of crashing waves.

Legend proclaims that it was from Egyncleugh Tower, perched above this deep gorge, that Queen Margaret was riskily lowered into a fishing boat to escape her enemies besieging the castle in 1462.

Now follow the fence line up to the castle entrance and join a footpath that encircles this 14th century stronghold. After viewing the splendid craggy northern end of the castle, retrace your steps to rejoin the shoreline route back to Craster.

LOW NEWTON-BY-THE-SEA (6 on map)

From the car park on the approach road to Low Newton, walk down to the square of old fishermen's cottages lining three sides of a green where - prior to the building of a sea wall in the 1940s - boats were hauled ashore during winter storms.

A National Trust information board gives information about the walks between Craster and Beadnell.

First, take the footpath behind the village square to Embleton Dunes and bird hides leading to Newton Pool Nature Reserve which in summer attracts migrant birds including sandpipers and greenshank.

It is also a favourite nesting area for black headed gulls, and some 30 different species of birds including mallard, coot, teal and mute swan.

Return along the beach to the village and take the footpath signposted to Beadnell. The path follows the rocky foreshore and after passing the Ministry of Defence installation reaches Newton Point.

Low Newton

Rounding the point there is a fine view looking north into Beadnell Bay. Follow the dune-top path above the small sandy beach in Football Hole bay then branch left on a path that follows an old stone wall and leads to Link House car park.

From here, walkers can either continue on into Beadnell Bay or take the road that leads up to High Newton and back to Low Newton.

BAMBURGH TO BUDLE BAY (4 on map)

From the roadside car park below Bamburgh Castle, take the footpath that leads uphill towards the castle and then drops down towards the beach.

Cross the dunes and set off in a northerly direction along the beach towards Harkess Rocks, where a low vertical rock face is decorated with a painting of a white stag. Agile walkers can keep to the rocky foreshore others may prefer to take the path which skirts around the landward side of the lighthouse.

From this point there is an excellent view towards Lindisfarne and the northern stretch of Ross Sands.

Cross the next sandy bay which leads up to Budle Point and turn into Budle Bay. Continue along the beach until reaching the remains of a small quay used until early this century to load boats with whinstone from nearby Kittling Hill quarry.

Climb into the dunes past a wartime gun emplacement, then turn left along a path on top of the dunes that follows the old quarry waggonway along the edge of Bamburgh golf course.

Continue along the path marked with yellow posts to the golf clubhouse, then join the road past the lighthouse which leads back to Bamburgh.

The shoreline north of Bamburgh.

ROSS BACK SANDS (2 on map)

This glorious 3-mile stretch of quiet sandy seashore, - part of the Lindisfarne National Nature Reserve - can be reached via the B1342 from Bamburgh or from the A1 along the road signposted to Elwick and Easington Grange. (A 1/2 mile north of Easington Grange farm, turn right for 1 mile to Ross).

Park on the roadside verge before reaching Ross Farm, walk along the road through the hamlet and then follow the footpath for 3/4 mile across farmland to the shoreline.

Summer flowers to be found in the dunes include viper's bugloss-with its bright blue flower spikes- and hound's tongue, a bushy, soft grey leafed plant with small wine red flowers.

Keep to the waymarked footpath leading up into the high dunes which offer a panoramic view of Holy Island to the north, the Farne Islands to seaward and Bamburgh Castle.

Once on the beach, either turn south for a 1-mile walk to the mouth of Budle Bay or north for a 2 mile beachcombing stroll up towards two needle-shaped stone navigational pillars.

A good place for the shell collector, 5 species of tern breed in this area and in late summer wading birds which return here from their Arctic breeding grounds include dunlin, bar-tailed godwits, grey plover, curlew, oystercatcher and redshank.

HOLY ISLAND - EASTERN SHORELINE (3 on map)

From the car park near the harbour, take the footpath which leads past the entrance to the castle and over the hill passing the walled garden originally created by Gertrude Jekyll.

The footpath joins a raised track - once used as a waggonway to carry limestone to the harbour - which curves seaward along the island's eastern shoreline towards the white pyramid shaped beacon at Emmanuel Head.

From Emmanuel Head follow a track over the dunes into Sandham Bay, the landing place in 793 of a Viking raiding party which ransacked and burned the abbey founded by Aidan.

Drop down to the beach and cross the bay to The Ness End, where grey seals can often be seen.

For an alternative, inland return route, take one of the numerous paths back through the network of dunes until reaching a fence marking the boundary between the nature reserve and farm land. Between the fields, a track known as the Straight Lonnen leads back to the village.

HOWICK HAVEN AND HOWICK DENE (7 on map)

Park on the roadside verge 1 mile east of Howick Hall, at Sea Houses Farm, where the coast road turns sharply left towards Craster.

Follow the coastal footpath signposted Boulmer 2½ miles down a gated track between fields which leads after ¾ mile to a small sandy bay where the Howick Burn runs into the sea.

A footbridge crosses the burn for walkers wishing to continue on to Boulmer.

But for a complete contrast to this rocky coastal scene, take the winding path that follows the burn up Howick Dene through attractive old woodland owned by the Howick Trustees.

A little way up the dene a sign indicates that while access is permitted, this is not a public right of way and the path is closed once a year on the second Wednesday in February.

This 1½ mile "Long Walk" between the sea and Howick Hall was the favourite of Charles, 2nd Earl Grey of Reform Bill fame, who lived here between 1801 and 1845 and was responsible for planting many of the trees seen today.

The path passes through a revolving gate in a deer fence erected to protect the many small trees and shrubs in the young woodland areas ahead.

Continue along the path as it leads up to a plantation and turns left along to a small lake created as a fish pond for the Hall in 1819. To follow the " Long Walk" continue straight on for some 600 yards until reaching a roadside gate near Howick Hall.

A shorter return route is offered by following a path along the edge of the fish pond to a revolving gate and turning right onto the road which leads back to the starting point of the walk.

(Howick Hall gardens opening times, see page 11)

WARKWORTH (8 on map)

From the old market square, Dial Place, go right along the edge of the churchyard and follow the narrow lane into St Lawrence Terrace which leads to Bridge Street. Turn left to the 14th century fortified bridge, where a footpath leads off to the left down to the riverside.

Keep to this riverside footpath which after passing beneath the castle is signposted to Mill Walk and Howlett Hall. Rowing boats can be hired here in summer months and from this tranquil stretch of the River Coquet there are inspiring views of the Percy stronghold towering above the wooded riverbank.

The footpath leads over a stile into an open field and on to a landing stage where a ferryboat operates on Wednesdays only to take visitors across the river to explore the famous Warkworth Hermitage. (See page 7)

Returning towards the village, take the footpath (near the rowing boat steps) that leads uphill to skirt the base of the castle walls before entering Castle Street and dropping downhill back to St. Lawrence's Church.

———————————

All the walks in this chapter are between 2 and 4 miles in length.

CHAPTER SIX

GOOD BEACH GUIDE

FAMILY BEACHES ideal for picnics, with safe bathing, easy access and convenient parking.

1. WARKWORTH DUNES

Access by minor road immediately north of river bridge, signposted "To beach". Free car park, picnic area and toilets located 300 yards from beach. Public bridleway leads down to dunes and seashore. This classic Northumberland beach has won numerous awards for cleanliness and water quality.

With fine views of Coquet Island, the beach stretches almost two miles between the Coquet estuary and Birling Carrs rocks. Good, safe bathing, on a gently shelving beach which has little seaweed, soft sand above high water line, and is sheltered by sand dunes.

2. ALNMOUTH

A minor road off the main street, signposted "To the beach" leads down to a large pay parking area near the old lifeboat houses adjoining the beach. Nearest toilets are across the links near the village golf club.

This l-mile beach running north from the Aln estuary is the winner of a Tidy Britain Group Seaside Award and while signs warn of dangerous currents in and near the estuary, the beach area furthest from the river mouth is safe for bathing.

3. EMBLETON

A road from the village leads after 2/3 mile to Dunstanburgh Castle Golf Course. There is limited roadside parking and pay parking at the golf club.

A path crosses the links - watch out for golfers - to the sand dunes bordering this first-rate beach which offers one of the most romantic views of Dunstanburgh Castle standing 1 1/2 miles to the south.

The 1-mile long beach is quite steeply shelved near the high water mark and this can cause an undertow dangerous for children and inexperienced swimmers.

4. BEADNELL BAY

Access to this 2-mile long, curving, sand dune fringed beach is from a large pay car park near Beadnell Harbour. This gently shelving beach offers safe bathing and the sheltered bay is popular with water sports enthusiasts.

A boat ramp leads from the car park onto the beach. Windsurf boards and canoes can be hired. Toilets located in car park.

Beadnell Bay.

5. SEAHOUSES- ST. AIDAN'S DUNES

Lying just off the coast road to the north of Seahouses, some free roadside parking is available. Bordered by National Trust protected dunes, this ³/₄ mile stretch of beach running up to Monks House Rocks offers fine views of the Farne Islands.

The beach is gently shelving and offers safe bathing. Nearest toilet facilities in Seahouses.

6. BAMBURGH

A fine beach stretches south from the castle to the coastguard look-out station. The large sand dunes offer many sheltered picnic areas. Pay parking is available in the large car park opposite the castle or at the links car park on the southern edge of the village. Toilets are located nearby.

Off the beach is the Islestone, and lying to the south is the main group of Farne Islands. Unless the sea is rough, bathing is safe from this 1¹/₂ mile long beach.

BEACHES OFF THE BEATEN TRACK - with limited parking.

7. ALNMOUTH DUNES

This botanically rich conservation area protected by the National Trust can be reached by walking north along the shoreline from Warkworth Dunes. Alternative access by car is via a poorly surfaced track, just over 1 mile south of the Hipsburn roundabout, marked with a footpath sign to Buston Links.

The track leads down to links near the dunes where there is a limited amount of parking space. Signs warn against bathing in or near the estuary. Please keep to established paths through the dunes which lead onto a superb stretch of quiet beach.

8. SEATON POINT

Follow the coast road north of Alnmouth past Foxton Golf Course, then towards Boulmer for 2¼ miles. A track leads off the road to the right by an emergency telephone box. There is space for a few cars to park here. A path leads down into a small sandy bay lying beneath the golf course which is bordered by Marden Rocks and Seaton Point.

The bay can also be reached on foot by walking north along the shoreline from Alnmouth beach. Bathing here is safe although seaweed can be a problem. The rock pools which edge the bay to north and south contain a wide variety of marine life.

9. LONGHOUGHTON

Follow the signposted road from the village to Low Steads. The farmer allows access across the private links but visitors are requested to place at least 20p into a fundraising honesty box for Longhoughton Church funds.

The private road runs for ½ mile beyond the farm to a metal gate through which cars can be parked on the grass banks above Howdiemont Bay. The next bay to the north is Sugar Sands, a secluded, sheltered beach which shelves quite steeply causing undertows that can be dangerous for swimmers.

Beyond Sugar Sands is the bay at Howick Burn mouth (see walk page 54) All three bays offer good opportunities to observe seabirds and for rockpool exploration. An area designated as a Site of Special Scientific Interest, Low Steads is protected under covenant by the National Trust.

———————

Walks along beaches at Holy Island, Ross Sands, North Bamburgh to Budle Bay, and Boulmer, and coastal paths at Howick Haven and Craster are featured in chapter five.

For access points to the foreshore between Bamburgh and Berwick at Fenham-le-Moor, Fenham Mill, Goswick and Cocklawburn - see pages 31.)

Bamburgh Castle peeps over the sand dunes to the south of the village.

The view south from Newton Haven.

CHAPTER SEVEN

SHIPWRECKS AND HEROES

Winter gales, sudden storms, dense fog and the powerful tides that sweep round Northumberland's rocky coastline and islands have combined to claim the lives of a great many seafarers.

Long ago, when navigational charts were rudimentary and, before the introduction of lighthouses and lifeboats, a passage through these dangerous waters struck dread into the hearts of many a mariner.

And in those far-off days, the misfortune of shipwreck victims was often the source of income for those living on the coast.

14th century records show that the monks living on Inner Farne collected substantial sums of money by claiming the salvage rights to vessels wrecked on the island.

In 1472 - a time when no love was lost between Northumbrians and Scots - the richly laden barge St Salvador, belonging to the Bishop of St. Andrews, foundered off Bamburgh.

Whether loss of life occurred is not recorded, but her rich cargo loaded in Flanders was certainly plundered and her wealthiest passenger, a Scottish abbot, was taken prisoner and released only after payment of an £80 ransom.

The toll of wrecks and lost lives mounted through the following centuries and in the 18th century Bamburgh Castle's trustee, Dr John Sharp, having witnessed the death of a ship's captain, who survived the sinking of his vessel only to contract pneumonia from sleeping in a damp bed in the village, provided accommodation and clothing in the castle for shipwreck survivors.

By 1770 he had also helped establish an ingenious hazard warning system to assist ships sailing through uncharted waters around the Farne Islands.

In foggy weather, a gun mounted in Bamburgh Castle's battlements was fired at 15 minute intervals and a bell in the south turret was rung to warn ships of their nearness to the islands.

Each night a light burned in the castle keep to give ships a bearing, and in times of storm two horsemen patrolled 8 miles of coastline. If they spotted a ship in difficulty, the alert was raised by firing a cannon to call out local men to help mount a rescue.

It was Dr Sharp who also asked local inventor, Lionel Lukin, to convert a fishing coble into a livesaving boat by fitting buoyancy air boxes to it. The boat was based at Mill Burn, Bamburgh in 1786 establishing what is claimed to be the first lifeboat station in the world.

The payment of a premium for saving lives initiated by Dr Sharp - a sum of £1 given to the first rescue boat to reach a shipwreck - continued to be paid until 1898.

Following his death in 1792, Dr Sharp's work was continued by the Lord Crewe Trustees who, in 1802 established a lifeboat station served by a 10-oared coble on Holy Island, and later set up the North Sunderland lifeboat station at Seahouses.

These independent, locally funded lifeboats were gradually integrated into the Royal National Lifeboat Institution, along with other lifeboats at Beadnell, Boulmer, Amble, Tweedmouth, Alnmouth and Craster.

Seahouses lifeboat around the turn of the century. Coxswain Michael Robson is sitting on the wheel.

The first self-righting lifeboat was bought by the Duke of Northumberland and based at Boulmer in 1852 but up to 1918 many of the coast's lifeboats remained sail powered and it was not until 1939 that each station had its own mechanically propelled lifeboat.

From the early days of the lifeboat service, the bravery of their volunteer crews and the vital support of their womenfolk who frequently helped launch the lifeboats from storm lashed beaches, resulted in the lives of many hundreds of seafarers being saved.

But disasters could not always be averted.

GRACE DARLING

In a northerly gale on the night of September 7, 1838, the 400 ton paddle steamer Forfarshire, bound for Dundee with a complement of 66 passengers and crew, struck Big Harcars and quickly broke up within sight of the Farne Islands' Longstone Lighthouse.

At first light Grace saw that a number of survivors had scrambled ashore onto Big Harcars and she and her lighthouse keeper father, William, determined to go to their aid. They launched their small coble and rowed half a mile through heavy seas to reach the survivors.

A contemporary painting of Grace Darling's rescue.

They rescued eight men and one woman and with the assistance of the fittest survivors managed to row the 21-foot coble back to the safety of Longstone.

Unaware that the survivors had been rescued, seven Seahouses fishermen - including Grace's brother William - put to sea in a coble to reach the wreck and were then forced to spend two days on Longstone until the storm abated.

A further nine people who had scrambled into a ship's lifeboat were later picked up safely many miles to the south but the remaining 48 passengers and crew perished.

This heroic rescue made 22 year old Grace a national heroine. Hundreds of articles, books and ballads were written about her brave deed, unsolicited gifts and honours poured in, but four years later, having steadfastly shunned all offers of fame and fortune, she died from TB.

An equally tragic loss of life occurred in July 1843 when the paddle steamer Pegasus hit Goldstone Rock midway between the Farnes and Holy Island. Only 6 of her 51 passengers and crew survived.

A chart compiled by Seahouses resident John Hanvey in the 1970s details the locations of 500 shipwrecks around the Farne Islands and along the coast between Holy Island and Beadnell.

As a consequence, the Holy Island and North Sunderland lifeboats in particular, have seen much active service.

For some time Holy Island boasted three lifeboat stations and the crews who manned the vessels based there between 1867 and 1968 were responsible for saving 336 lives.

Records displayed in the North Sunderland lifeboat station at Seahouses harbour reveal that lifeboats stationed there have saved 368 lives.

The Golden Coast and Islands of NORTHUMBERLAND